Alfred's Basic Piano Lil

Piano

Repertoire Book
Level 4

Willard A. Palmer • Morton Manus • Amanda Vick Lethco

This book may be assigned at the student's first lesson in Lesson Book 4 of ALFRED'S BASIC PIANO LIBRARY. The pieces are coordinated PAGE by PAGE with Lesson Book 4, and should be assigned according to the instructions given in the upper right corner of the first page of each selection. Any piece may be assigned at any time after the student has completed the indicated pages, thereby avoiding difficulty with concepts not yet introduced. Problem-free lessons result from careful selection of appropriate materials.

OVERLAPPING CONCEPTS, indicated in the upper left corner of the first page of each piece, refer not only to the reinforcement of the exact principles introduced in the corresponding pages of the Lesson Book, but also to concepts previously introduced that are now being re-emphasized.

The pieces in this Repertoire Book are attractive compositions by outstanding musicians from the 17th century to the present. These selections meet the requirements at this level for piano festivals, auditions and competitions. The authors strongly recommend that students often participate in recitals and other performance opportunities.

This book may also be used to provide enjoyable sight reading material or as a supplement to any other method book of similar level. The variety of pieces is appealing and will be helpful in developing each student's musical and technical ability. The pleasure of playing this music will provide motivation for practicing and performing.

Cover Illustration by David Silverman
Back row: Sergei Prokofiev, Hector Berlioz, Dmitri Shostakovich, Gustav Mahler, Peter Ilyich Tchaikovsky, Giuseppi Verdi
Middle row: Franz Schubert, George Frideric Handel, Claude Debussy, Frédéric Chopin, Arnold Schönberg, Franz Liszt
Front row: Igor Stravinsky, Johannes Brahms, Johann Sebastian Bach, Ludwig van Beethoven, Wolfgang Amadeus Mozart, Franz Joseph Haydn

2

Contents

OVERLAPPING CONCEPTS

Key of F major
⁶⁄₈ time signature
Overlapping pedal
RH extensions

*Use after TARANTELLA in
LESSON BOOK 4 (pages 2–3).*

Johann Philipp Kirnberger, famous German theorist and composer, studied with
J.S. Bach in Leipzig. He later became a court musician for Frederick the Great.

Fanfare

Johann Philipp Kirnberger
(1721–1783)

Andante moderato

Eighth note triplet
RH extensions
LH melodic octaves
Staccato & legato

Use after HAUNTED HOUSE (pages 4–5).

Franz Joseph Haydn, one of the most famous composers of the Classical period, wrote many works for keyboard, as well as symphonies, string quartets, operas, masses and songs.

Allegro

Franz Joseph Haydn
(1732–1809)

Use after HAUNTED HOUSE (pages 4–5).

Key of D minor
Eighth note triplets
Broken chords (both hands)
LH crossing over RH
LH clef changes

Cornelius Gurlitt, German organist and composer, taught at the Hamburg Conservatory. This piece is a fine example of his attractive piano miniatures, for which he is best known.

The Ocean

Cornelius Gurlitt
(1820–1901)

6

LH root position & 1st inversion triads
Pedaling
Accents
LH harmonic 7th

Use after THE HOKEY-POKEY (pages 6–7).

Samuel Maykapar, Russian pianist, composer and teacher, studied in Vienna with a very famous teacher, Theodor Leschetizky. His best known compositions are short, imaginative pieces for piano.

Prelude

Samuel Maykapar
(1867–1938)

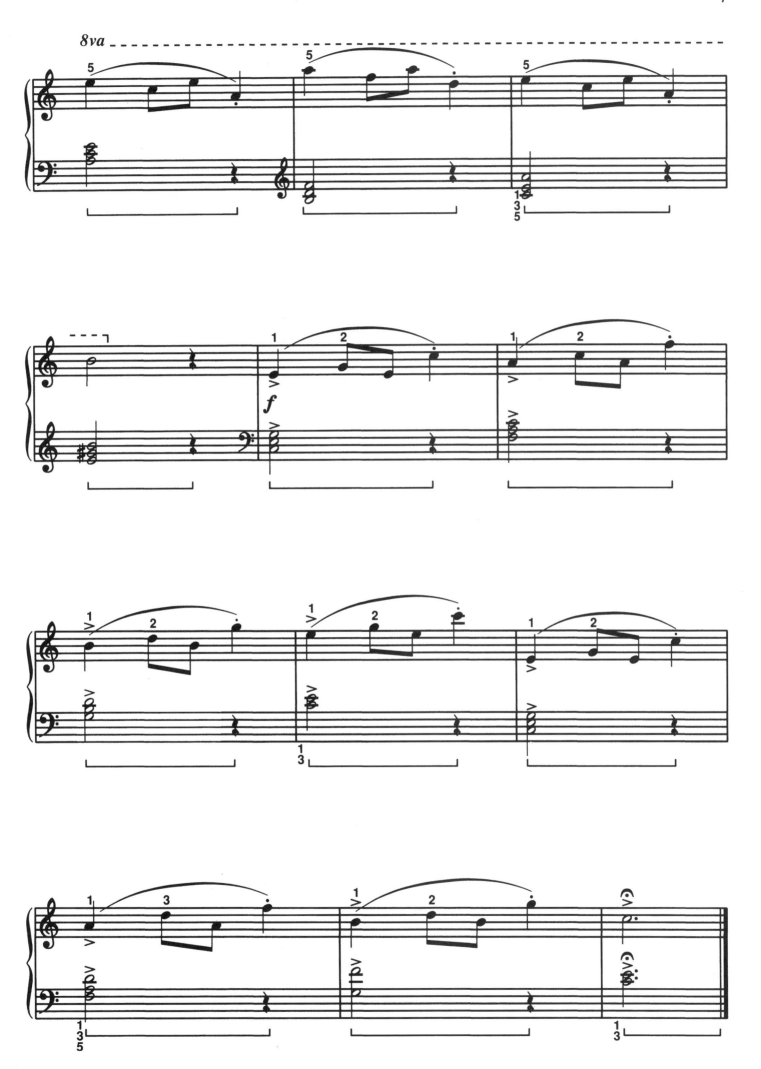

Use after PRELUDE IN A MINOR (pages 8–9).

Key of A minor
RH 1st inversion triads
$\frac{2}{4}$ time signature

Dmitri Kabalevsky, Russian pianist and composer, taught at the conservatory in Moscow. He composed many attractive and exciting pieces for young students. This *Toccatina* is one of his best known short compositions.

Toccatina

Dmitri Kabalevsky
(1904–1987)

Triads in all positions
Overlapping pedal

Use after TRIADS IN ALL POSITIONS (page 14).

Joachim Neander, 17th century Dutch composer, organist and harpsichordist, wrote many keyboard and vocal pieces. This chorale is typical of the church music of his time.

Chorale

Adagio

Joachim Neander
(1650–1680)

Use after FAREWELL TO THEE (page 15).

Triads in all positions
Overlapping pedal
Finger substitution
Arpeggiated chords

Carl Reinecke, German pianist and composer, studied with his father, who inspired him to become one of the leading musicians in the great musical city of Leipzig.

Prelude in C Major

Carl Reinecke
(1824–1910)

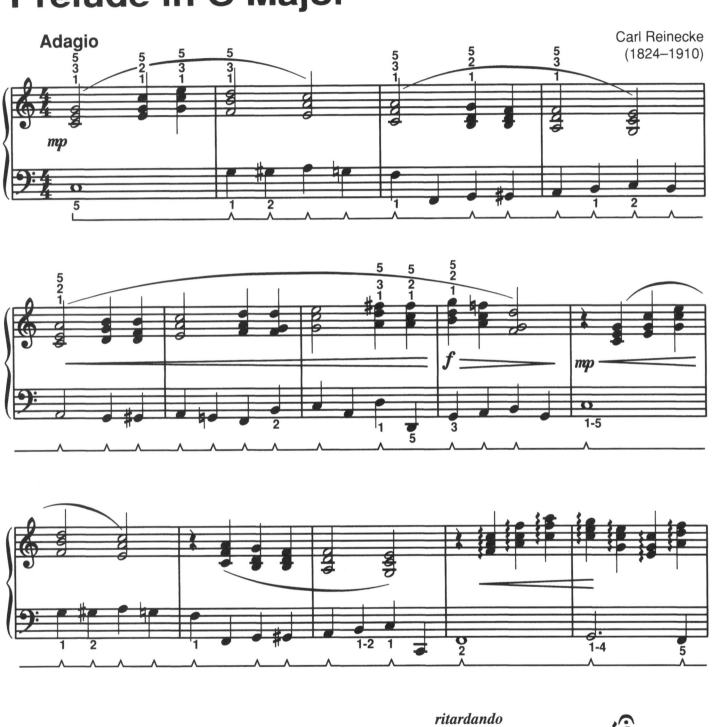

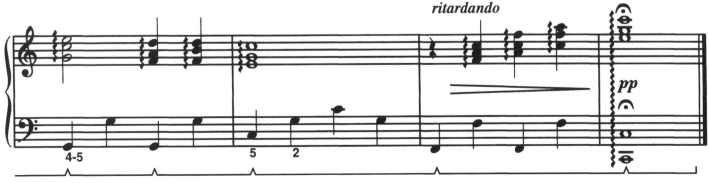

| Primary chords in G major |
| Repeated harmonic & melodic intervals |
| G triad in all positions |

Use after FAREWELL TO THEE (page 15).

Louis Streabbog, Belgian composer, pianist and teacher, was actually named Gobbaerts, but he preferred spelling his name backwards on hundreds of his educational piano compositions, many of which continue to be popular with teachers and students.

On the Green

Louis Streabbog
(1835–1886)

Syncopation
LH triad inversions
Accents

Use after CALYPSO HOLIDAY! (page 19).

Calypso Rhumba

Willard A. Palmer and
Amanda Vick Lethco

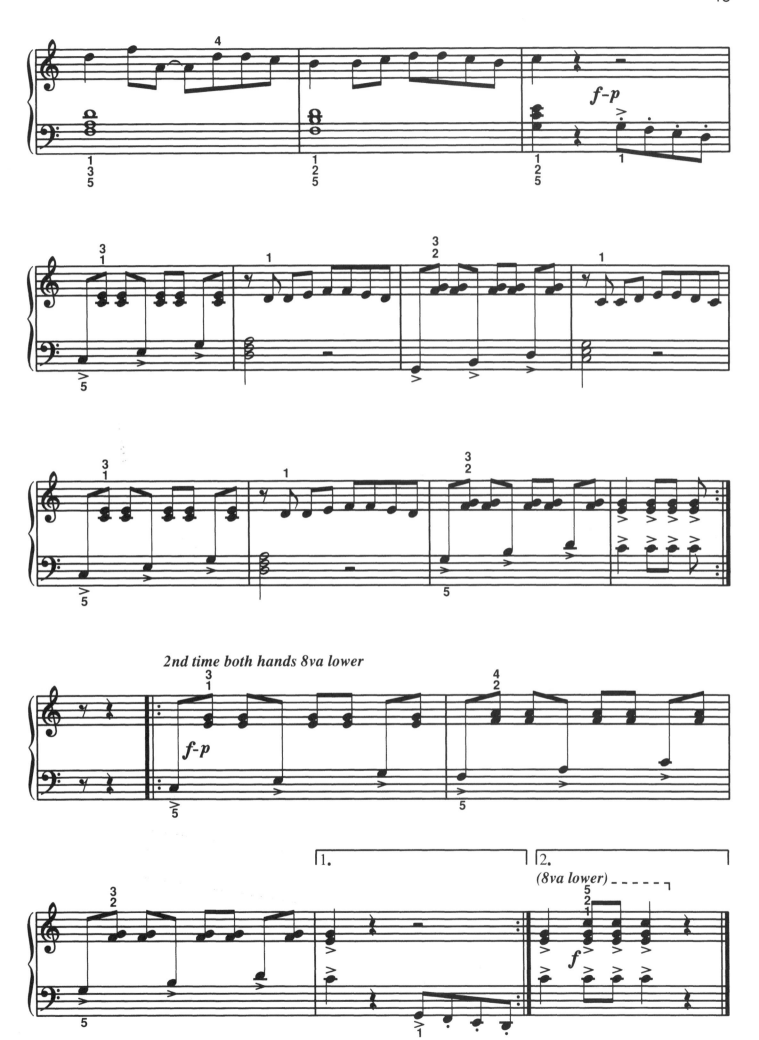

> Key of D minor
> Syncopation
> Common time
> Tenuto* (see footnote)

Use after CALYPSO HOLIDAY (page 19).

Béla Bartók, Hungarian pianist and composer, was fascinated with the unusual accents and rhythms of his native Hungarian folk music. This is a fine example of how he used some of these unusual features in creating short and exciting piano pieces.

Rhythmic Dance

Béla Bartók
(1881–1945)

Allegro deciso*

* *Deciso* indicates decisive style.

** ♩ indicates tenuto: hold the note for full value.

Use after POMP AND CIRCUMSTANCE (pages 20–21).

> Two-part writing
> RH broken chords
> LH harmonic intervals
> "Finger pedaling"* (see footnote)

Franz Joseph Haydn was court musician to three generations of princes at the Esterhazy palace in Eisenstadt, Austria, which is 30 miles from Vienna. He became a friend of Wolfgang Amadeus Mozart. Later, Haydn became one of Beethoven's teachers.

Country Dance

Franz Joseph Haydn
(1732–1809)

* "Finger pedaling" — Holding the lowest LH note while playing higher ones.

Two-part writing
$\frac{6}{8}$ time signature
LH extension

Use after POMP AND CIRCUMSTANCE (pages 20–21).

Anton Diabelli, Austrian composer and music publisher, was born near Salzburg, but spent most of his life in Vienna, where he taught piano and guitar. His name is still widely known because of an outstanding set of 33 variations Beethoven composed, based on one of Diabelli's themes. This tarantella is an especially interesting example of the many short educational piano pieces that Diabelli wrote and published.

Tarantella

Anton Diabelli
(1781–1858)

Allegro

Use after SWINGING SEVENTHS (page 23).

Key of D major
LH 7th chords
RH scale patterns
Accents
Tenuto

Ludwig van Beethoven, one of the greatest musicians in history, was born in Bonn, Germany, but lived most of his life in Vienna. He composed great masterworks in the form of symphonies, concertos, quartets, variations and sonatas. He was a brilliant pianist and was famous for his ability to improvise on any theme presented to him. His Ninth Symphony, based on Schiller's *Ode to Joy*, was performed by Leonard Bernstein with the Berlin Symphony Orchestra when the Berlin wall was torn down.

German Dance

Ludwig van Beethoven
(1770–1827)

Use after AMERICA, THE BEAUTIFUL (page 25).

> Inversions of triads & 7th chords
> Overlapping pedal
> $\frac{2}{4}$ and $\frac{6}{8}$ time signatures

In this piece by Gurlitt, the theme is varied by using broken treble chords. The theme and variation form has been used by composers for several centuries.

Theme and Variation

Cornelius Gurlitt
(1820–1901)

Variation

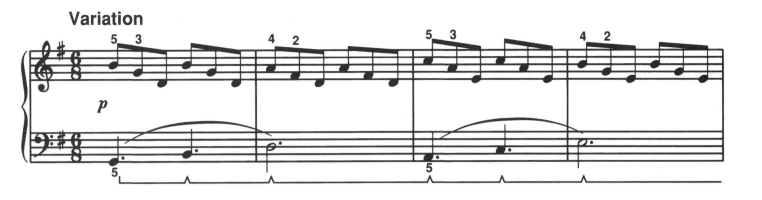

Use after WAVES OF THE DANUBE (page 28–29).

Key of E minor
Two-part writing
Overlapping pedal
Chord inversions

Peter Ilyich Tchaikovsky, one of the most highly acclaimed Russian composers, wrote symphonies, concertos, operas, overtures and piano pieces. His ballet, *The Nutcracker*, is traditionally performed during the Christmas season throughout the world. Van Cliburn, one of America's most famous pianists, won his first international recognition when he took first place in a competition in Russia, in which he played a Tchaikovsky piano concerto.

In Church

KEY OF E MINOR
Key Signature: 1 sharp (F#)

Peter Ilyich Tchaikovsky
(1840–1893)

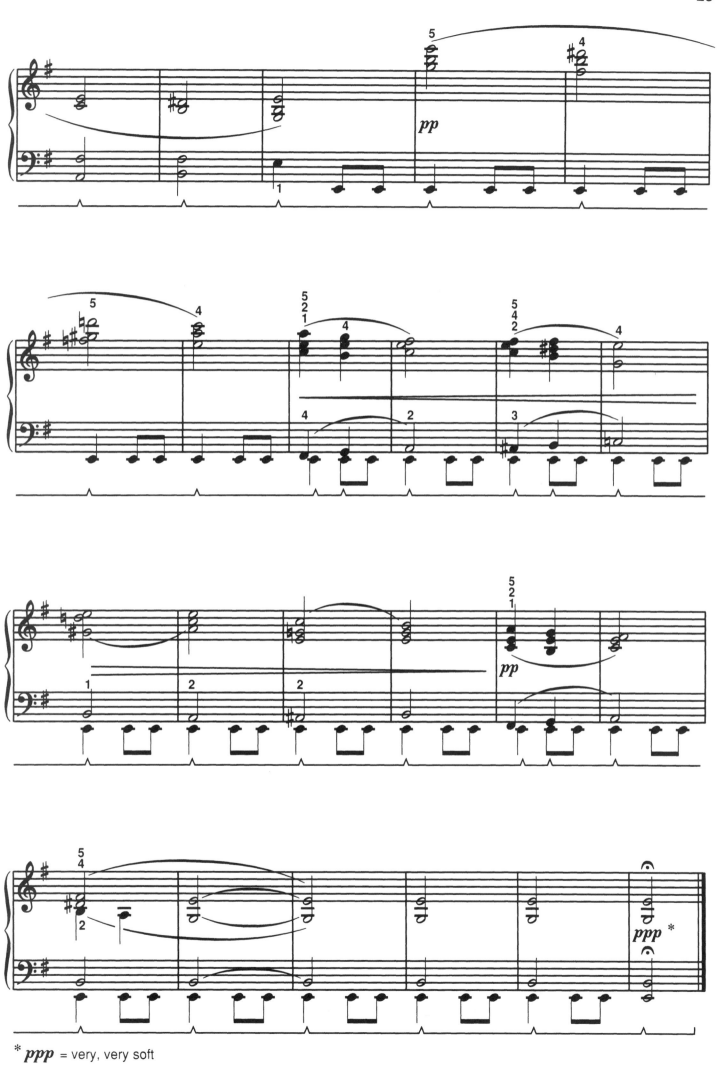

* **ppp** = very, very soft

Use after GYPSY DANCE (page 31).

Key of E minor
Sixteenth notes
⅜ time signatures

Muzio Clementi, Italian composer, pianist, music publisher and piano manufacturer, was adopted by a British gentleman when he was a child. He spent most of his long life in London. His piano method was very popular, and Beethoven recommended it. This is one of the pieces from his method.

Spanish Dance
"Guaracha"

Muzio Clementi
(1752–1832)

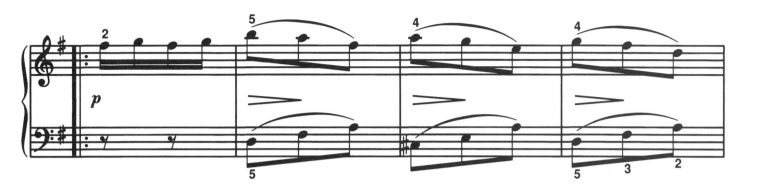

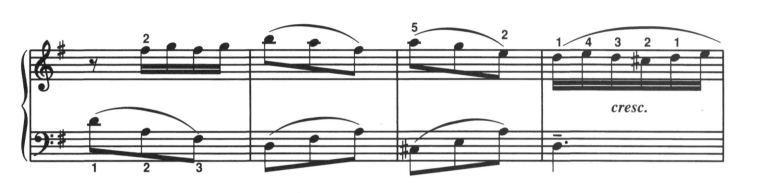

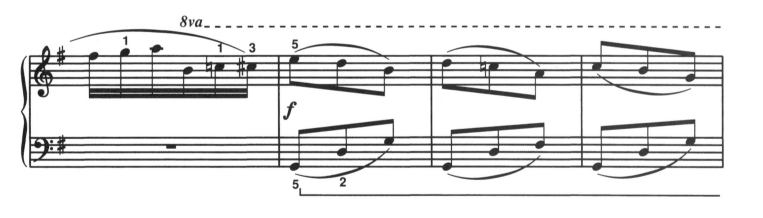

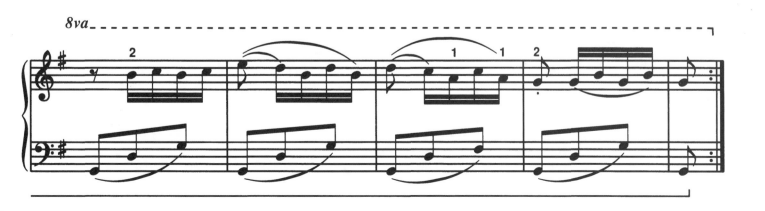

> Sixteenth notes
> LH melodic octaves
> Staccato
> Accents

Use after MUSETTE (pages 32–33).

Leopold Mozart was not only famous for nurturing the phenomenal talent of his son, Wolfgang Amadeus Mozart, but also for having been an excellent composer, a renowned violinist, and court composer in the service of the Archbishop of Salzburg, Austria.

Bourlesq *

Leopold Mozart
(1719–1787)

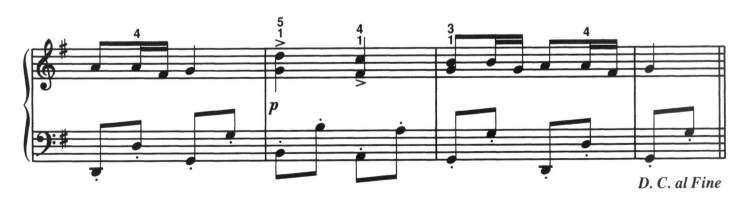

D. C. al Fine

* *Bourlesq.* = Old French spelling for "burlesque," a playful or comical dance.

| Key of D major |
| Dotted eighths & sixteenths |
| RH 1 under 2, 3 over 1 |

Use after BATTLE HYMN OF THE REPUBLIC (pages 34–35).

Daniel Gottlob Türk, German organist, composer and theoretician, was a professor at the University of Halle. This piece, which imitates the call of a horn and its echo, is characteristic of the many miniatures he wrote for piano students.

The Hunting Horn
and the Echo

Daniel Gottlob Türk
(1756–1813)

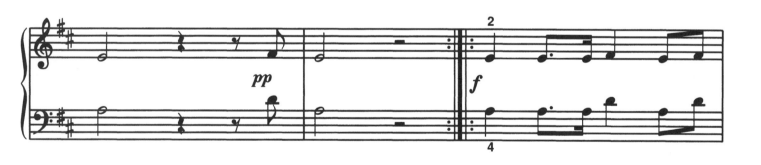

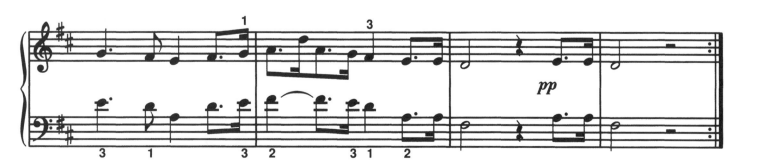

Use after THE MAGIC PIPER (page 37).

Key of B♭ major
Sixteenth notes
3/8 time signature
Staccato & legato

Samuel Maykapar taught piano at the St. Petersburg Conservatory in Russia. He played many successful concerts in Russia, Germany and Austria. He wrote instruction books for piano students, along with many excellent short compositions, such as this one.

The Music Box

KEY OF B♭ MAJOR
Key Signature: 2 flats (B♭ & E♭)

Allegro moderato
Play both hands 8va throughout

Samuel Maykapar
(1867–1938)

Use after SPINNING WHEEL (page 41).

Key of G minor
Two-part writing
LH extensions & broken chords
Pedaling

Peter Ilyich Tchaikovsky composed *OLD FRENCH SONG* for his *Album for the Young*, a collection of short piano pieces dedicated to his young nephew.

Old French Song

Peter Ilyich Tchaikovsky
(1840–1893)

KEY OF G MINOR
Key Signature: 2 flats (B♭ & E♭)

D. S. 𝄋 *al Fine*

Use after COMEDIAN'S DANCE (pages 46–47).

Changing fingers on repeated notes
Eighth note triplets
Two-part writing
Broken LH & RH chords
7th chords

This piece imitates the sound of the woodpecker. Rapid changing of fingers on the same note is an important keyboard technique for pianists. It is not difficult to master if you begin very slowly, keeping the wrist and arm relaxed, and very gradually increase speed.

The Woodpecker

Louis Streabbog
(1835–1886)

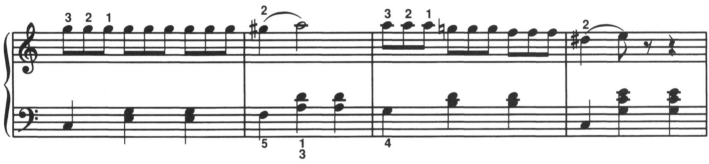

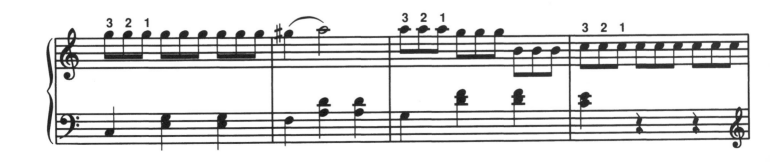

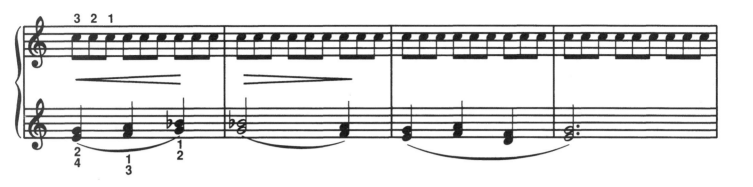

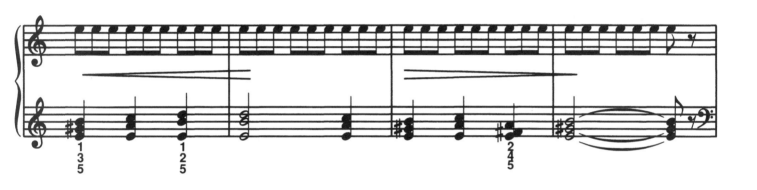